WILLIAMS-SONOMA
E S S E N T I A L S

MUSTARDS

GENERAL EDITOR
CHUCK WILLIAMS

RECIPES
ANN CREBER

PHOTOGRAPHY
PHILIP SALAVERRY

WILLIAMS-SONOMA
Founder & Vice President:
   Chuck Williams

WELDON OWEN INC.
President: John Owen
Publisher: Wendely Harvey
Managing Editor: Jill Fox
Consulting Editor: Norman Kolpas
Design & Illustration: Brenda Duke
Editorial & Design Assistant:
   Marguerite Ozburn
Recipe Assistants: Cathie Graham,
   Janet Lodge
Proofreader: Meredith Phillips
Indexer: ALTA Indexing Service
Production: Stephanie Sherman,
   James Obata
Photography Assistant:
   David Williams
Food Stylist: Bruce Yim
Food Stylist Assistants:
   Barbara Bragle, Tim Scott
Prop Stylist: Amy Glenn

Production by:
Mandarin Offset, Hong Kong
Printed in China

A Weldon Owen Production

WILLIAMS-SONOMA ESSENTIALS
Conceived and produced by:
Weldon Owen Inc.
814 Montgomery Street
San Francisco, CA 94133
Phone number: (415) 291-0100
Fax number: (415) 291-8841
In collaboration with:
Williams-Sonoma
100 North Point Street
San Francisco, CA 94133

Copyright © 1994 Weldon Owen Inc.
All rights reserved, including the rights
of reproduction in whole or in part in
any form.

Library of Congress
Cataloging-in-Publication Data:
Creber, Ann.
   Mustards / general editor, Chuck
Williams ; recipes, Ann Creber ;
photography, Philip Salaverry.
      p.   cm. -- (Williams-Sonoma
essentials)
   Includes index.
   ISBN 1-875137-19-X
   1. Cookery (Mustard) 2. Mustard
(Condiment)   I. Williams, Chuck.
II. Title. III. Series.
TX819.M87C74 1994
641.6'384--dc20   94-66
                                      CIP

ACKNOWLEDGMENTS
The publishers would like to thank
the following people and organiza-
tions for their assistance in lending
props for photography: Paul Bauer,
Inc.; Bethanie Brandon Design;
Virginia Breier Gallery; Clouds;
Cookin'; Cyclamen Studios, Julie
Sanders Designer; Missy Hamilton-
Backgrounds; Sue Fisher King; Mimi
Koch-Backgrounds; Susan Pascal;
Dan Schuster; Tesoro; WilkesHome
at Wilkes Bashford.

WEIGHTS AND MEASURES
All recipes include customary U.S.
and metric measurements. The metric
conversions are based on a standard
developed for these books and have
been rounded off. Actual weights
may vary. Unless otherwise stated,
the recipes were designed for
medium-sized fruits and vegetables.

CONTENTS

MUSTARD
E S S E N T I A L S

Several species of the *Brassica* plant, collectively known as mustard, have been cultivated for five millennia. Native to Asia and Europe, this pungent spice was used by ancient Chinese and Greek cooks and its seed found in Egyptian pyramids. Today mustard highlights a range of savory foods.

Mustard is sold as seeds, powder and in prepared blends. Different plant varieties produce powerful whole black seeds, slightly milder brown seeds and mild white seeds. Mustard powder is blended from brown and white seeds. Blends combine powder or seeds, various liquids and seasonings.

Store seeds and powder in airtight containers at cool room temperature up to a year. Refrigerate mustard blends up to six months.

MUSTARD POWDER

Mix mustard powder with seasonings and liquid to make any number of mustard blends. The flavor possibilities are unlimited, depending on the liquid and seasonings used. Stir mustard blends into dressings, sauces and glazes, or use them as condiments for meat or poultry.

Some basic principles apply when mixing mustard powders: While water promotes development of mustard's pungent flavor enzymes, acidic vinegars, wine and beer retard them, toning down flavor. Never mix mustard powders with boiling liquid because the heat blocks the reaction, yielding a bland to bitter mixture.

If time allows, refrigerate mustard blends for one or more days, which allows them to further develop their flavors, before using in a recipe.

RUSSIAN SALAD

The sweetness of Russian Mustard adds interest to this clever use of leftover chicken and pork.

- ½ lb (8 oz / 250 g) mixed cold cooked roasted pork and chicken, cubed
- 2 beets, steamed, peeled and diced
- 4 potatoes, peeled, boiled and diced
- 2 sour gherkins, diced
- ½ cucumber, peeled and diced
- 2 eggs, hard-cooked, shelled and chopped
- 2 tablespoons mayonnaise
- 2 tablespoons Russian Mustard
  White wine vinegar
- 2 teaspoons chopped fresh dill

Place the meat onto individual plates and arrange the vegetables and eggs around it. In a mixing bowl combine the mayonnaise, Russian Mustard and sufficient vinegar for sharpness. Stir in the dill. To serve, spoon the mayonnaise mixture over the meat.

RUSSIAN MUSTARD

- ½ cup (2½ oz / 75 g) mustard powder
- 1 cup (8 oz / 250 g) sugar
- ¼ teaspoon salt
- ¾ cup (6 fl oz / 180 ml) warm water
- 1 tablespoon vegetable oil
- 1 teaspoon white wine vinegar

In a bowl combine the mustard powder, sugar and salt. Gradually add the water to make a paste. Mix well. Stir in the oil and vinegar. Add more water, if needed, for a smooth consistency. Cover and chill. The mustard may be stored in the refrigerator up to 1 week.

Serves 4

CHEESE AND WALNUT MUFFINS

Serve these savory muffins still warm from the oven with cheese or butter.

1   cup (5 oz / 155 g) each *whole-wheat (wholemeal) flour and all-purpose (plain) flour*
3   *teaspoons baking powder*
1   *teaspoon mustard powder*
½   *cup (2 oz / 60 g) chopped walnuts*
½   *cup (2 oz / 60 g) grated Cheddar cheese*
    Freshly ground pepper
1   *cup (8 fl oz / 250 ml) milk*
1   *egg, lightly beaten*

Preheat an oven to 450°F (230°C). Grease or paper muffin tins. In a large bowl sift together the flours, baking powder and mustard powder. Stir in the walnuts, cheese and pepper to taste. Make a well in the center and pour in the milk and egg. Mix until ingredients are barely blended. Fill the muffin tins three-quarters full. Bake until a tooth-pick inserted in the center of a muffin comes out clean, about 20 minutes.

Makes 12 muffins

ITALIAN SAUSAGES

Use a variety of sausages for this robust buffet dish.

- 3 red bell peppers (capsicums), roasted, peeled, stemmed, seeded and deribbed
- 6 sausages
- 1 cup (4 oz / 125 g) each *black and green olives*
   Fresh herbs

Cut peppers into bite-sized pieces. Grill sausages until cooked through, about 10 minutes. To serve, arrange meat on a platter surrounded by peppers and olives. Garnish with herbs. Use Italian Mustard for dipping.

ITALIAN MUSTARD

- 1 small white onion
- 6 whole cloves
- 1 cup (8 fl oz / 250 ml) Italian dry white wine
- ¾ cup (6 oz / 185 g) mustard powder

Pierce onion with cloves. In a saucepan combine wine and onion. Cover and simmer 15 minutes. Strain wine into a small bowl. Cool. Gradually stir in mustard powder until smooth.

Serves 6

DIJON MUSTARD

Since the 14th century, Dijon, France, has been famed for mustard. That fame grew greater in the mid-19th century, when Maurice Grey invented a machine to streamline manufacture and, with Auguste Poupon, began the brand Grey Poupon.

Under French law, true Dijon mustard comes only from that region. Dijon-style mustard is a similar blend that has been prepared elsewhere. Either way, the mustard combines black or brown seeds, wine grape juice, wine, vinegar, water, salt and other flavorings. Briefly aged in oak, it is pale yellow, fairly hot and sharp—an ideal condiment or savory seasoning.

In addition, Dijon mustard can be flavored with a range of ingredients to add more zest to recipes. (Flavored Mustard recipes begin on page 26.)

TUNA TARTARE

Use a variety of greens such as arugula, endive and chervil as the base for this summer appetizer.

- ½ lb (250 g) very fresh tuna or salmon fillet, skin removed
- ⅓ cup (3 fl oz/80 ml) sour cream
- 1 tablespoon Dijon mustard
  Juice of 2 fresh limes
  Freshly ground pepper
- 1 ripe but firm avocado
  Fresh greens
- 1 small white onion, finely chopped or grated
- 1 oz (30 g) red fish roe

Chop the tuna very finely. Cover and chill. In a medium bowl, whip together the sour cream, Dijon mustard and a teaspoon of the lime juice. Add pepper to taste. Cover and chill. Halve, pit, peel and slice the avocado, brushing the slices with the remaining lime juice. To serve, arrange the greens, onions and tuna on individual plates. Surround with the avocado and fish roe. Top with the sour cream mixture.

Serves 2–3

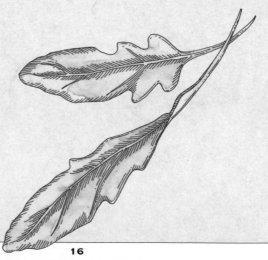

VEGETABLE MELANGE

Try this for a change when you're bored with traditional salads.

- 1 large red (Spanish) onion
- 2 each *yellow and red bell peppers (capsicums), roasted, peeled, stemmed, seeded, deribbed and julienned*
- 12 *red cherry tomatoes, halved*
- 6 *small yellow pear tomatoes, halved*
  Fresh basil leaves
- 6 *black olives*

Slice onion lengthwise from tip to root, blanch and pat dry. To serve, arrange the onion, peppers, tomatoes, basil and olives on individual plates. Top with Dijon-Basil Dressing.

DIJON-BASIL DRESSING

- 1 *tablespoon Dijon mustard*
- 2 *tablespoons basil vinegar*
- 3 *tablespoons virgin olive oil*
  Salt and freshly ground pepper

In a small bowl whisk together the Dijon mustard, vinegar and olive oil. Add salt and pepper to taste.

Serves 6

TAPENADE CRISPS

Purchase puff pastry from the frozen food section of a market.

- 1 cup (5 oz / 155 g) black olives, pitted and chopped
- 4 canned anchovy fillets, chopped
- 2 teaspoons capers, rinsed
- 3 teaspoons Dijon mustard
- 2 teaspoons fresh lemon juice
- 2 tablespoons light olive oil
  Freshly ground pepper
- 2 sheets puff pastry, about 12 inches (30 cm) square, thawed

Preheat an oven to 400°F (200°C). Grease a baking sheet. In the work bowl of a food processor purée the olives, anchovy fillets, capers, Dijon mustard, lemon juice and olive oil. Add pepper to taste. Spread the mixture evenly over the pastry sheets, leaving a rim of about ½-inch (12-mm) all around. Roll pastry. Freeze until pastry is just firm enough to slice into ½-inch (12-mm) thick slices. Arrange slices on baking sheet. Bake until golden brown, about 25 minutes, turning over the last 5 minutes.

Makes about 48 crisps

GOUGERE WITH MUSTARD

Originating in the French countryside, gougère are cheese-filled pastries, which are served as an appetizer or salad accompaniment.

1 cup (5oz/155 g) all-purpose (plain) flour
½ teaspoon salt
¼ cup (2 oz/60 g) unsalted butter
1 cup (8 fl oz/250 ml) water
4 medium eggs
½ cup (2 oz/60 g) finely diced Cantal or Cheddar cheese
1 tablespoon Dijon mustard
1 tablespoon freshly grated Parmesan cheese

Preheat an oven to 425°F (220°C). Grease a baking sheet and the inside of the outer rim of a springform pan. Sift together the flour and salt. In a large saucepan combine the butter and water and bring to a boil. Add the flour all at once and beat vigorously with a wooden spoon until the mixture forms a ball and leaves the sides of the saucepan. Cool 5 minutes. Add the eggs one at a time, beating after each addition with an electric beater until smooth. Stir in the Cantal cheese and Dijon mustard. Place the prepared rim of the springform pan (base removed) onto the baking sheet. Spoon the mixture around the inner edge of the rim, making about 8 piles. Sprinkle with the Parmesan cheese. Bake until well-risen and golden, 40–50 minutes. To serve, cut into chunky pieces. Serve hot.

Serves 4

EGGPLANT WITH GOAT CHEESE

To eliminate their bitter juices, sprinkle eggplant slices with salt and drain in a colander about 30 minutes.

- 4 *slender (Asian) eggplant*
  (aubergine)
  Salt
- 3 *tablespoons olive oil*
- 2 *tablespoons Dijon mustard*
- 2½ *oz (75 g) goat cheese (chèvre)*
  Fresh herbs, chopped
- 2 *tomatoes, peeled and finely*
  chopped

Preheat a broiler (griller). Cut each eggplant into thin slices lengthwise. In a frying pan, heat olive oil and lightly brown eggplant on each side. Place slices on a baking sheet. Spread one side of each with a little Dijon mustard and a light coating of mashed goat cheese. Broil until cheese is well browned, 7–10 minutes. To serve, arrange slices on serving platter. Garnish with herbs and tomatoes.

Serves 4

BEEF IN BOURBON

An overnight soak in this mustard marinade makes any cut of beef more tender and flavorful.

- *4   5 oz (155 g) ¾-inch (2-cm) thick beef fillets*
- *3   tablespoons bourbon whiskey*
- *2   tablespoons light soy sauce*
- *1   tablespoon brown sugar*
- *1   small onion, finely chopped*
- *1   tablespoon Dijon mustard*
- *1   teaspoon Worcestershire sauce*

Arrange the fillets in a shallow casserole dish. In a small bowl mix together the bourbon whiskey, soy sauce, brown sugar, onion, Dijon mustard and Worcestershire, blending into a marinade. Pour the marinade over the fillets. Cover and refrigerate 12 hours, turning the meat often to ensure it is well-marinated. Prepare a fire in a barbecue grill or preheat a broiler (griller). Drain and reserve the marinade. Grill the fillets over hot coals or broil until cooked as preferred. To serve, place meat onto individual plates. Top with the reserved marinade.

Serves 4

PORK MEDALLIONS

Because a generous quantity of mustard is an essential ingredient in this sauce, use a mild version of Dijon, especially the first time you try this. Prepare the sauce first and keep it warm while cooking the medallions.

2   lbs (1 kg) pork tenderloin, cut into 3-inch (7.5-cm) pieces

¼   cup (2 fl oz / 60 ml) vegetable oil

3   large red bell peppers (capsicums), stemmed, seeded, deribbed and cut into ¼-inch x 3-inch (6-mm x 7.5-cm) strips

4   bottled artichoke hearts, quartered

Gently flatten the pork. In a frying pan heat 2 tablespoons of the oil. Add the pepper strips and artichoke hearts and, stirring often, cook 5 minutes. Remove vegetables from pan and keep warm. In the same pan heat the remaining oil. Brown the pork 1 minute per side and then cook about 4 minutes per side. To serve, arrange the pork on individual plates and top with Mustard Béchamel. Garnish with the bell peppers and artichoke hearts.

MUSTARD BECHAMEL

¼   cup (2 oz / 60 g) unsalted butter

2   tablespoons all-purpose (plain) flour

1   cup (8 fl oz / 250 ml) milk, scalded

¼   cup (2 fl oz / 60 ml) dry white wine

¼   cup (2 oz / 60 g) Dijon mustard

1   tablespoon whole-grain mustard

In a heavy pan over medium heat melt 2 tablespoons of the butter. Add the flour. Cook 2 minutes, stirring constantly. Whisk in the milk and wine. Remove from the heat and whisk in the mustards and remaining butter. Keep warm until serving time.

Serves 4

Like any spice, mustard marries well with other seasonings. No surprise then that flavored mustards spring up in such great variety. Some of the flavored mustards described on this and the following three pages are featured in the recipes beginning on page 30.

Other mustards are designed as spreads for savory breads, condiments for meats and to further enhance recipes that call for simpler mustards. Use creativity and culinary sense when pairing mustards and recipes.

Make flavored mustards from scratch using mustard powder or by adding seasonings to prepared Dijon mustard. Dijon, with its strong but smooth taste, makes an ideal base. Either way, these mustards must be prepared in advance of use to allow the flavors to meld.

TARRAGON MUSTARD

1 cup (8 oz / 250 g)
  Dijon mustard
3 tablespoon
  chopped
  fresh
  tarragon
2 teaspoons
  white wine
  vinegar
2 teaspoons
  honey

In a bowl combine the Dijon mustard, tarragon, vinegar and honey. Whisk until blended. Spoon into a sterilized container and seal. Refrigerate 2 days. Makes 1 cup (8 oz / 250 g).

CHILI MUSTARD

⅔ cup (5 oz/160 g)
   Dijon mustard
⅓ cup (3 oz/90 g)
   whole-grain mustard
1 teaspoon
   chili
   powder
½ teaspoon paprika
1 tablespoon cider
   vinegar
1 tablespoon virgin
   olive oil

In the work bowl of a
food processor or
blender combine the
mustards, chili pow-
der and paprika. Process
30 seconds. Add the
vinegar and oil. Process
30 seconds. Spoon into
a sterilized container
and seal. Refrigerate
2 weeks. Makes 1 cup
(8 oz/250 g).

CHIVE MUSTARD

1 cup (8 oz/250 g)
   Dijon mustard
1 tablespoon whole-
   grain mustard
3 tablespoons very
   finely chopped fresh
   chives
1 teaspoon chive
   vinegar

In a bowl combine the
mustards, chives and
vinegar. Whisk until
blended. Spoon into
a sterilized container
and seal. Refrigerate
8 hours. Makes 1 cup
(8 oz/250 g).

DILL MUSTARD ✓

¾ cup (6 oz / 188 g) Dijon mustard

3 tablespoons hot mustard

2 tablespoons finely chopped fresh dill

1 table-spoon dried dill

½ teaspoon dill seeds

1 tablespoon olive oil

3 tablespoons white wine vinegar

⅓ teaspoon freshly ground pepper

In a bowl combine the mustards, dills, olive oil, vinegar and pepper. Whisk until blended. Spoon into a sterilized container and seal. Refrigerate 1 week. Makes 1 cup (8 oz / 250 g).

SHALLOT MUSTARD ✓

¾ cup (6 oz / 188 g) Dijon mustard

¼ cup (2 oz / 63 g) whole-grain mustard

4 large shallots, finely chopped

1 tablespoon cider vinegar

1 tablespoon olive oil

In a bowl combine the mustards, shallots, vinegar and oil. Whisk until blended. Spoon into a sterilized container and seal. Refrigerate 24 hours. Makes 1¼ cups (10 oz / 310 g).

HONEY MUSTARD

3 tablespoons mustard
   powder
1½ tablespoons whole-
   grain mustard
1 teaspoon ground
   cardamom
1 teaspoon chopped
   fresh mint leaves
¼ cup (2 fl oz/60 ml)
   cider vinegar
¼ cup (2 fl oz/60 ml)
   light olive oil
2 tablespoons honey
3 teaspoons Scotch
   whisky
2 tablespoons all-
   purpose (plain) flour

In the work bowl of a
food processor or
blender combine the
mustards, cardamom and
mint. Process 30 sec-
onds. Add the vinegar,
oil, honey and whisky.
Process 30 seconds.
Add the flour. Process
30 seconds. Spoon into
a sterilized container
and seal. Refrigerate
1 week. Makes 1 cup
(8 oz/250 g).

GREEN PEPPERCORN MUSTARD

1 cup (8 oz/250 g)
   Dijon mustard
3 tablespoons whole
   green peppercorns
1 tablespoon white
   wine vinegar
1 tablespoon olive oil

In the work bowl of a
food processor or blender
combine the Dijon
mustard, peppercorns,
vinegar and oil. Process
until smooth. Spoon into
a sterilized container
and seal. Refrigerate
1 week. Makes 1¼ cups
(10 oz/310 g).

PESTO MUSTARD

¾ cup (6 oz/188 g)
   Dijon mustard
½ cup (½ oz/15 g)
   fresh basil leaves
¼ cup (1 oz/39 g) pine
   nuts, toasted
2 tablespoons grated
   Parmesan cheese
2 tablespoons olive oil
1 garlic clove, peeled

In the work bowl of a
food processor or
blender combine the
Dijon mustard, basil,
pine nuts, cheese, oil
and garlic. Process until
smooth. Spoon into a
sterilized container
and seal. Refrigerate
24 hours. Makes 1½
cups (12 oz/375 g).

POTATO AND BEAN SALAD

Serve this salad at room temperature.

- 2 *lb (1 kg) small or new potatoes*
- 1 *lb (500 g) fresh or frozen fava (broad) beans*
- ½ *cup (4 fl oz / 125 ml) purchased French dressing*
- ⅓ *cup (3 fl oz / 80 ml) heavy (double) cream*
- 3 *teaspoons Chive Mustard (recipe on page 27)*
  Salt and freshly ground pepper
- 4 *slices bacon, fried and crumbled*
- 2 *tablespoons chopped fresh chives*

Steam or boil potatoes until tender. If larger potatoes are used, cut into chunks. Cook beans in boiling water until tender, about 15 minutes. Drain. In a small bowl whisk together the French dressing, cream and Chive Mustard. In a large bowl combine the potatoes and beans. Pour on the dressing. Salt and pepper to taste. Mix to ensure potatoes are evenly coated. To serve, transfer to a serving platter. Garnish with the bacon and chives.

Serves 6

GREEN BEAN SALAD

Any string beans—Kentucky
Wonders, Blue Lakes and even Asian
Longs—work well in this mix.

- 2 lb (1 kg) green beans, trimmed
- 3 tablespoons red wine vinegar
- 1 tablespoon Chili Mustard
   (recipe on page 27)
   Salt and freshly ground pepper
- ½ cup (4 fl oz / 125 ml) virgin
   olive oil
- 2 small red (Spanish) onions,
   thinly sliced
- ¾ cup (3 oz / 90 g) toasted pine nuts
- 2 cups (2 oz / 60 g) salad greens
- 1 head radicchio, leaves separated

Steam the beans until tender, about
6 minutes. In a small bowl combine the
vinegar and Chili Mustard. Salt and
pepper to taste. Whisk in the olive oil
until well blended. In a large bowl
combine the beans, onions and two
thirds of the pine nuts. Pour in the
vinegar mixture and toss well. To
serve, arrange the greens and radicchio
on a platter. Top with the bean mixture
and remaining pine nuts.

Serves 6

This recipe was designed for a 10- to 12- pound smoked ham, but any pre-cooked ham will work splendidly.

12 lb (6 kg) smoked ham

¼ cup (2 oz/60 g) brown sugar

1 tablespoon Honey Mustard (recipe on page 29)

1 8 oz (250 g) can sliced pineapple

2 tablespoons whole cloves

2 cups (16 fl oz/500 ml) sweet sherry or sweet white wine

Preheat an oven to 350°F (180°C). Peel skin and fat from ham, if necessary. In a small bowl combine sugar and Honey Mustard. Rub mixture over the ham. Place ham into a baking pan. Drain pineapple and reserve juice. Top ham with pineapple slices. Pierce ham with cloves. Pour sherry and reserved juice over ham. Bake about 3 hours, basting regularly with pan juices. To serve, remove cloves and cool slightly prior to carving. Delicious hot or cold.

Serves 8–10

BURGUNDIAN HAM

An excellent use for leftover ham, this traditional French dish makes a quick and easy supper.

- *½ lb (250 g) cooked ham, diced*
- *3 tablespoons unsalted butter*
- *5 eggs*
- *¼ cup (1½ oz / 45 g) all-purpose (plain) flour*
- *2 cups (16 fl oz / 500 ml) milk, warmed*
- *1 tablespoon Dijon mustard mixed with ½ teaspoon chopped fresh thyme*
- *Salt and freshly ground pepper*

Preheat an oven to 350°F (180°C). In a frying pan sauté the ham in 1 tablespoon of the butter, 4–5 minutes. Transfer to a 2-quart (64-fl oz / 2-l) ovenproof dish. In a large bowl whisk together the eggs and flour until smooth. Whisk in the milk and Dijon mustard. Salt and pepper to taste. Pour over ham and mix. Dot with the remaining butter. Bake until custard is set and golden brown, 35–40 minutes. Cool several minutes before serving.

Serves 4

HONEYED RACK OF LAMB

- 3 lb (1.5 kg) rack of lamb
- 2 tablespoons Honey Mustard (recipe on page 29)
- 1½ teaspoons grated fresh ginger
- 1½ teaspoons chopped fresh rosemary
- 1 cup (8 fl oz/250 ml) unsweetened apple cider
- ½ cup (4 fl oz/125 ml) rich beef stock
  Freshly ground pepper
  Fresh rosemary sprigs

Preheat an oven to 450°F (230°C). Trim excess fat from lamb. In a small bowl mix the Honey Mustard, ginger and rosemary. Rub mixture evenly over the meat. Place in a shallow roasting dish. Pour cider and stock over the meat. Roast 30–40 minutes, basting with pan juices after 10 minutes. Transfer lamb to a carving board and cover with foil to retain heat. Strain pan juices into a small, heavy saucepan. Boil until reduced to ¾ cup (6 fl oz/180 ml). Add pepper to taste. To serve, spoon sauce onto individual plates. Carve lamb into chops and arrange on top. Garnish with rosemary.

Serves 4–6

HALIBUT IN TARRAGON

Use halibut or any firm white-fleshed, large-boned, slightly fatty fish for this simple recipe.

4 6 oz (185 g) halibut steaks (cutlets)
⅓ cup (3 fl oz/80 ml) virgin olive oil
1½ tablespoons lemon juice
1 tablespoon Tarragon Mustard
    (recipe on page 26)
    Salt and freshly ground pepper
    Fresh tarragon sprigs
    Lemon slices

Put fish in a shallow glass dish. In a medium bowl blend the oil, lemon juice and Tarragon Mustard. Add salt and pepper to taste. Brush three-quarters of the mixture over the fish. Cover and chill several hours. Preheat a broiler (griller). Broil fish until flesh is opaque, turn over, baste with reserved oil mixture and cook until other side is done. Do not overcook. To serve, garnish with tarragon and lemon slices.

Serves 4

SALMON WITH MUSTARD SAUCE

While the cream adds flavor, it also adds calories to this otherwise rather low-calorie main dish.

- *4 6 oz (185 g) salmon steaks*
- *3 tablespoons fresh lemon juice*
- *2 tablespoons white wine*
- *⅓ teaspoon mustard powder*
- *1 tablespoon olive oil*
- *2 tablespoons unsalted butter*
- *2 tablespoons all-purpose (plain) flour*
- *¼ cup (2 fl oz / 60 ml) white wine vinegar*
- *½ cup (4 fl oz / 125 ml) chicken stock*
- *1 tablespoon Dill Mustard (recipe on page 28)*
- *1 tablespoon sugar*
- *1 egg, beaten*
- *2 tablespoons heavy (double) cream*
  Lettuce leaves
  Fresh dill

Put the salmon into an ovenproof dish. In a small bowl whisk together the lemon juice, wine, mustard powder and olive oil. Pour over the salmon, reserving 1 tablespoon. Marinate 30 minutes, turning once. Preheat a broiler (griller). Broil until cooked through, about 5 minutes per side. In the top of a double boiler blend together the butter and flour and cook 2 minutes. Add the vinegar, stock, Dill Mustard and sugar and, stirring constantly, cook 5 minutes. Remove from the heat and add the egg, whisking vigorously. If desired, stir in the cream. To serve, arrange the lettuce leaves on a serving platter and sprinkle with reserved marinade. Place the salmon onto the lettuce. Top with the sauce. Garnish with the dill.

Serves 4

TOURNEDOS OF BEEF

The addition of asparagus spears, artichoke hearts and tangy Mustard Béarnaise sauce enhances the appeal of this popular dish.

- 4   5 oz (155 g) market (ribeye) steaks, about 1-inch (2.5-cm) thick, cut into 3-inch (7.5-cm) rounds
- ¼   cup (2 oz/60 g) unsalted butter
- 4   slices white bread, about 1-inch (2.5-cm) thick, cut into 3-inch (7.5-cm) rounds
- 8   asparagus spears, trimmed and blanched
- 4   bottled artichoke hearts, halved

Preheat a broiler (griller). Broil the steaks as desired, about 5 minutes per side for medium rare. In a frying pan melt the butter and brown the bread. Set aside. Heat the asparagus and artichoke hearts, adding a little more butter to the pan, if necessary. To serve, place the bread onto individual plates. Place the steaks on bread and top with Mustard Béarnaise. Arrange asparagus and artichoke hearts on top. Serve immediately.

MUSTARD BEARNAISE

- 1   cup (8 oz/250 g) unsalted butter
- 2   shallots, finely chopped
- ¼   cup (2 fl oz/60 ml) white wine vinegar
- 1   tablespoon tarragon vinegar
     Salt and white pepper
- 4   egg yolks
- 1   tablespoon Tarragon Mustard (recipe on page 26)
- 2   teaspoons finely chopped fresh tarragon
     Fresh lemon juice

In a saucepan melt the butter, skim off white froth and set aside. In another saucepan combine shallots, vinegars and salt and pepper to taste. Reduce until the liquid has almost evaporated. Add 2 tablespoons of water to the reduction and pour into the top of a double boiler. Add the egg yolks, whisking until creamy. Beat in the Tarragon Mustard. Remove from heat and whisk one minute. Gradually pour in the butter, constantly whisking. Stir in the tarragon and a few drops of lemon juice. Serve warm.

Serves 4

HOT MUSTARD

With its sharp, tangy taste and pleasurable, sinus-clearing sensation, nothing compares to hot mustard. Purchase commercial blends or make hot mustard by blending powdered brown and white seeds with water. Add horseradish, pepper or Japanese wasabi for more flavor.

Use hot mustard as a condiment and seasoning. Either way, a little goes a long way. The amounts in this chapter provide a medium heat level. However, even that amount may take some getting used to. Consider lessening the amount of hot mustard until you are ready for its special pungency. As 19th-century English mustard tycoon Jeremiah Colman is said to have observed, his company's profits were found not in the mustard people ate but in what they left on their plates.

COUNTRY PEA AND HAM SOUP

The last-minute addition of mustard adds pungency to this sturdy soup. 𝒱

- *1   small smoked ham hock*
- *1½ cups (10 oz / 330 g) dried green split peas*
- *2   white onions, finely chopped*
- *1   sprig thyme*
- *1   fresh bay leaf*
- *1   teaspoon black peppercorns Salt*
- *2   tablespoons hot mustard*

In a large saucepan combine the ham hock, peas, onions, herbs and peppercorns. Cover with water and simmer very gently until meat and peas are tender, 2–2 ½ hours. Add more water, if necessary. Remove the hock from the saucepan. When cool enough to handle easily, strip the skin and meat from the hock. Chop the meat and return it to the saucepan. Reheat the soup. Salt to taste. Stir in the hot mustard just before removing from the heat. Serve hot.

Serves 6

HAM RAMEKINS

Any single-serving baking dish can be called a ramekin. Typically they are made of porcelain and look like small soufflé dishes. They are made to go from oven to table.

Butter, for ramekin preparation
⅛ lb (60 g) finely chopped smoked ham
1 egg, separated
2 tablespoons milk
1½ teaspoons hot mustard
2 teaspoons finely chopped fresh parsley
Freshly ground pepper

Preheat an oven to 350°F (180°C). Butter 2 or 3 ramekins. In a medium bowl mix together ham, lightly beaten egg yolk, milk, hot mustard, parsley and pepper. In a separate bowl whip egg white until stiff and fold into ham mixture. Pour into prepared ramekins to three-quarters full. Bake 20 minutes. Serve immediately.

Serves 2–3

BARBECUED SHRIMP

Saffron rice is an excellent counterpoint to this spicy barbecue sauce.

- 2 *lb (1 kg) uncooked shrimp (prawns)*
- ¼ *cup (2 oz / 60 g) unsalted butter*
- 2 *tablespoons green bell pepper (capsicum), stemmed, seeded, deribbed, and chopped*
- 1 *tablespoon hot mustard*
- 1 *tablespoon mango chutney*
- 2 *teaspoons purchased barbecue sauce*
- 2 *teaspoons chopped fresh parsley*
- ⅓ *teaspoon cayenne pepper*
- 1 *teaspoon Worcestershire sauce Tabasco (hot red pepper) sauce Salt*
- ½ *cup (4 fl oz / 125 ml) heavy (double) cream*
- 1 *lemon, quartered*

Prepare a fire in a barbecue grill. Shell and devein the shrimp, leaving head and tail intact. In a saucepan melt the butter, add the green pepper and sauté 1 minute. Add the hot mustard, chutney, barbecue sauce, parsley, cayenne and Worcestershire. Add Tabasco and salt to taste. Simmer until the sauce thickens slightly. Remove mixture from heat and add the cream. Cook the shrimp over hot coals, brushing often with the sauce during cooking. Cook only until flesh of shrimp becomes opaque, 1–2 minutes per side. To serve, remove the shrimp from the grill and brush with any remaining sauce. Garnish with the lemon quarters.

Serves 4–6

GLAZED CHICKEN

You'll know that this chicken is cooked when the juices run clear after being pierced with a fork.

- 4 *chicken thighs or half breasts, about 5 oz (155 g) each*
- 2 *tablespoons hot English mustard*
- 1 *tablespoon Dijon mustard*
- ¼ *cup (2 oz/60 g) superfine (castor) sugar*
- 3 *tablespoons fresh lemon juice*
- 2 *tablespoons light olive oil*
- 1 *tablespoon fresh orange juice*
- 2 *teaspoons soy sauce*
- 1 *tablespoon light (single) cream*

Preheat a broiler (griller). Place the chicken into a baking dish, skin side down. In a bowl combine the mustards, sugar, lemon juice, olive oil, orange juice, soy sauce and cream. Beat until smooth. Baste the chicken with one quarter of the glaze. Broil 15 minutes, basting with another quarter of the glaze after seven minutes. Turn, baste with half the remaining glaze and cook 20–30 minutes, basting with remaining glaze after 15 minutes.

Serves 4

CHICKEN IN CREAMY SAUCE

1 2½ lb (1.25 kg) chicken, cut
   into pieces
2 tablespoons all-purpose
   (plain) flour
   Salt and freshly ground pepper
2 tablespoons olive oil
2 tablespoons unsalted butter
¼ lb (125 g) fatty bacon
   (speck), diced
2 small white onions, chopped
1 bouquet garni
⅔ cup (5 fl oz / 160 ml) each dry
   white wine and chicken stock
1 tablespoon hot mustard
1¼ cups (10 fl oz / 310 ml) light
   (single) cream

Dredge the chicken pieces in the flour.
Salt and pepper to taste. In a frying pan
heat together the oil, butter and fatty
bacon. Add the chicken and sauté until
golden brown, 3–4 minutes per side.
Add onions, bouquet garni, wine and
stock. Cover and cook until the chicken
is tender, about 1¼ hours. Remove the
chicken and bouquet garni. Skim the
fat from the surface of the sauce.
Whisk in the hot mustard and cream.
To serve, place the chicken onto individual plates. Top with the sauce.

Serves 4

CRUSTY CORNED BEEF

A corned cut of beef is ideal for this recipe. If the meat is very salty, soak it overnight in the refrigerator and then discard the water.

- 4 lb (2 kg) corned (brined) beef
- 4 tablespoons (2 oz/60 g) brown sugar
- 2 tablespoons cider vinegar
- 1 onion, roughly chopped
- 1 fresh bay leaf
- 2 sprigs fresh thyme
- 6 peppercorns
- 1 orange, halved
- 1/4 cup (2 oz/60 g) hot mustard
- 1 1/2 cups (3 oz/90 g) bread crumbs
- 3 tablespoons chopped fresh parsley
- 1/4 cup (2 oz/60 g) unsalted butter, melted
- Freshly ground pepper
- Mustard Béchamel (recipe on page 24)

Trim all the fat from the beef. Place the meat into a large pot with 2 tablespoons of the brown sugar, vinegar, onion, bay leaf, thyme, peppercorns and orange. Add water to cover. Bring to a boil. Reduce heat, cover and simmer gently until meat is tender when pierced with a fork, about 1 1/2 hours. Remove from the heat and cool meat in the cooking liquid. Preheat an oven to 350°F (180°C). Remove meat, pat dry and place into a baking dish. Strain and reserve 1 1/2 cups (12 fl oz/375 ml) of the cooking liquid. Spread the hot mustard evenly over the meat. In a bowl combine the reserved liquid, bread crumbs, remaining brown sugar, parsley, butter and pepper to taste. Mix well. Press mixture over meat. Bake until crisp and golden, about 30 minutes. To serve, slice the meat onto individual plates. Top with the Mustard Béchamel.

Serves 6–8

During the production of whole-grain mustard, all or some of the brown and white seeds are left completely or partially uncrushed, leaving the blend with a crunchy texture.

The experience of eating whole-grain mustard—dabbed on meat or swirled into a soup, sauce, or glaze—stands apart. The taste is intriguing, as the seeds pop open when eaten, releasing their delicious flavor.

As with Dijon mustard, many flavored whole-grain mustards are available, from French red-wine Bordeaux to robust German beer blends to Scandinavian dill mustards.

The recipes in this chapter call for plain whole-grain mustard. In general, use plain for cooked recipes; for condiments, let your personal preferences and sense of adventure prevail.

CUCUMBER BISQUE

Designed to be served cold, this bisque makes a deliciously refreshing repast on a hot afternoon.

- *6 tablespoons (3 oz/90 g) unsalted butter*
- *3 green (spring) onions, chopped*
- *2 large cucumbers, peeled, seeded and finely chopped*
- *3 cups (24 fl oz/750 ml) chicken stock*
- *2 tablespoons all-purpose (plain) flour*
- *1 tablespoon whole-grain mustard*
- *1 cup (8 fl oz/250 ml) sour cream*
- *2 medium cucumbers, 1 seeded and diced, 1 sliced*
- *2 tablespoons chopped chives*
  Salt and freshly ground pepper

In a saucepan melt two thirds of the butter, stir in the onions and chopped cucumber and cook until the onions are transparent. Add the stock and simmer, uncovered, 20–30 minutes. Cool. Transfer to the work bowl of a food processor or blender and purée. In a saucepan melt the remaining butter and stir in the flour. Pour in the puréed mixture and whole-grain mustard and, while stirring, heat until slightly thickened but not boiling. Refrigerate at least 4 hours. Stir in two thirds of the sour cream, diced cucumber and chives. Salt and pepper to taste. To serve, ladle into individual bowls. Garnish with the remaining cucumber and sour cream.

Serves 6

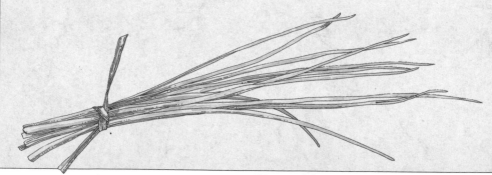

HERBED POLENTA DIAMONDS

This dish can be used as a substitute for bread at any meal or topped with tomato sauce in lieu of pasta.

3¾ *cups (30 fl oz / 935 ml) milk*
 1 *onion, halved*
 1 *bay leaf*
    Peppercorns
 ¾ *cup (4 oz / 125 g) polenta*
    (yellow cornmeal)
    Salt and freshly ground pepper
 ½ *cup (2 oz / 60 g) freshly grated*
    Parmesan cheese (plus a little
    extra)
 3 *tablespoons unsalted butter*
 2 *tablespoons finely chopped mixed*
    fresh herbs
 2 *teaspoons whole-grain mustard*

Preheat an oven to 350°F (180°C). In a saucepan, combine the milk, onion, bay leaf and peppercorns to taste and slowly bring to a boil. Strain the milk, discard the other elements and return milk to the saucepan. Sprinkle in polenta, stirring constantly to avoid lumps. Add salt and pepper to taste. Cook slowly until mixture is thick, about 15 minutes. Stir in cheese, 2 tablespoons of the butter, herbs and mustard. Mix until smooth. Spread evenly on a greased baking sheet to about a ½-inch (12-mm) thickness. Cool, then chill in refrigerator 1–2 hours. When the polenta is cold, cut into diamonds, dot with the remaining butter and sprinkle with extra cheese. Place on baking sheet. Bake until golden brown, about 5 minutes on each side. To serve, transfer to a serving platter.

Serves 6

SAVORY BRUSSELS SPROUTS

The addition of tangy mustard transforms predictable Brussels sprouts into a special-occasion vegetable.

- 1½ lbs (750 g) Brussels sprouts, trimmed
- ½ cup (4 oz / 125 g) unsalted butter
- 1 tablespoon whole-grain mustard
- 1½ teaspoons fresh lemon juice
  Freshly ground pepper
- 1 cup (2 oz / 60 g) fresh whole-wheat (wholemeal) bread crumbs
  Zest of 1 fresh lemon

Steam Brussels sprouts until tender, about 15 minutes. In a small saucepan melt half the butter. Blend in mustard, lemon juice and pepper to taste. In a frying pan melt remaining butter and sauté bread crumbs, stirring constantly until golden. To serve, transfer sprouts to a heated dish. Pour butter mixture over the sprouts and mix lightly. Sprinkle with hot bread crumbs. Garnish with lemon zest.

Serves 6–8

MUSTARD STEAK

Simple roasted vegetables complement the zesty flavor of the marinated meat.

- 1 tablespoon whole-grain mustard
- 2 teaspoons crushed peppercorns
- 1 teaspoon Dijon mustard
- 1 clove garlic, minced
- 1 lb (500 g) sirloin (rump) steak
- 2 tablespoons port wine

In a bowl combine whole-grain mustard, peppercorns, Dijon mustard and garlic; mix well. Spread the mustard mixture on both sides of the meat. Set steak in glass baking dish. Sprinkle the wine over the top of the steak. Marinate, lightly covered, at least 2 hours at room temperature or overnight in the refrigerator. Preheat a broiler (griller) or prepare a fire in a barbecue grill. Broil or barbecue the steak about 5 minutes on each side, depending on thickness, for medium rare.

Serves 3–4

COLD BEEF WITH ASPARAGUS

Best cooked the day it is to be served, this dish makes an excellent lunch.

- 3   tablespoons whole-grain mustard
- 3   lb (1.5 kg) beef tenderloin (fillet), fat removed
       Freshly ground pepper
- 3   tablespoons heavy (double) cream
- ½   cup (4 oz / 125 g) mayonnaise
- 24   asparagus spears, trimmed

Brush the mustard over the beef and let stand 1 hour. Preheat an oven to 400°F (200°C). Put the beef into a greased baking dish. Pepper to taste. Roast 40 minutes for medium rare. Remove from dish and cool without refrigerating. In a mixing bowl combine the pan drippings, cream and mayonnaise. Cook asparagus in boiling water 3 minutes. To serve, slice the beef onto a serving platter with the asparagus. Top with the mayonnaise mixture.

Serves 6

BAKED HAM WITH CRANBERRY-MUSTARD GLAZE ✓

Ever-succulent ham is even more delectable with the addition of this sweet mustard glaze.

- 1   5 lb (2.5 kg) cooked ham
- 1   can (16 oz / 500 g) whole cranberry sauce
- ¾   cup (6 oz / 185 g) firmly packed brown sugar
- 2   tablespoons whole-grain mustard
- 1   tablespoon grated orange zest
- ½   teaspoon ground cinnamon

Preheat an oven to 300°F (150°C). Peel all the skin and as much fat as possible from the ham. Put into a baking dish. Press the cranberry sauce through a strainer into a saucepan. Add the sugar, mustard, orange zest and cinnamon and mix well. Warm over low heat, stirring often. Cool slightly before spooning onto the ham, spreading as evenly as possible. Bake 1 hour, basting several times during the cooking. To serve, transfer to a serving platter.

Serves 8–10

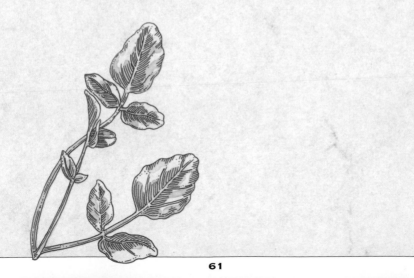

SMOKED HAM WITH BISCUITS

This creamy spread is an excellent use for any leftover cooked ham. Smoked ham is cooked in the curing process. If ham isn't available already ground, finely chop the meat by hand or in a food processor.

- ½ lb (250 g) smoked ham, finely ground
- ½ cup (4 oz / 125 g) unsalted butter, softened
- 1 tablespoon whole-grain mustard

In a medium bowl beat together the ham, butter and mustard until well mixed. Pack into a crock and chill. To serve, bring to room temperature. Spread on the Sour Cream Biscuits.

SOUR CREAM BISCUITS

- 2 cups (10 oz / 315 g) all-purpose (plain) flour
- 1 teaspoon baking powder
- 1 teaspoon baking soda (bicarbonate of soda) Salt
- 1⅓ cups (11 fl oz / 330 ml) sour cream

Preheat an oven to 450°F (230°C). Sift together the flour, baking powder, baking soda and salt to taste into a bowl. Make a well in the center. Gently mix in cream to make a very light dough. On a lightly floured board, pat dough into a rectangle about 1-inch (2.5-cm) thick. Cut into 16 small rectangles. Place onto a lightly floured baking sheet and bake until risen and golden topped, about 15 minutes. Split each biscuit in two before serving.

Serves 4

I N D E X